Published in North America in 2014 by Owlkids Books Inc.

Published under the title *Le temps qui passe* © 2010 Éditions Milan.

Owlkids Books acknowledges the financial support of the Canada Council for the Arts, the Ontario Arts Council, the Government of Canada through the Canada Book Fund (CBF) and the Government of Ontario through the Ontario Media Development Corporation's Book Initiative for our publishing activities.

Published in Canada by
Owlkids Books Inc.
10 Lower Spadina Avenue
Toronto, ON M5V 2Z2

Published in the United States by
Owlkids Books Inc.
1700 Fourth Street
Berkeley, CA 94710

Estellon, Pascale
[Temps qui passe. English]
    It's about time : untangling everything you need to know
about time / Pascale Estellon.

Translation of: Le temps qui passe.
Translation by Sarah Quinn.
ISBN 978-1-77147-006-3 (bound)

    1. Time--Juvenile literature. 2. Time measurements--Juvenile
literature. I. Title. II. Title: Temps qui passe. English

QB209.5.E8813 2014   j529   C2013-904511-2

Library of Congress Control Number: 2013946678

Manufactured in Shenzhen, Guangdong, China, in October 2013, by WKT Co. Ltd.
Job #13CB0513

A   B   C   D   E   F

Publisher of Chirp, chickaDEE and OWL
www.owlkidsbooks.com

IT'S ABOUT TIME

I'm Lily!

And I'm Jacob!

Untangling Everything You Need to Know About Time

Pascale Estellon

You can't see it,
you can't hear it,
you can't touch it,
you can't smell it,
but you can count it…

What is it?

It's time!

Come on...
Let's go see what time is all about!

1

one
second

What is a second?

It's how long it takes you to turn this page,
or how long it takes to do a little doodle,
like this one:

One second is just a tiny little instant.
It's how long it takes to count to

1.

1

one
minute

What is a minute?

It's a lot longer than a second!
It's how long it takes to count to
60.

Turn the page and count with us...

1	2	3	4	5
6	7	8	9	10
11	12	13	14	15
16	17	18	19	20
21	22	23	24	25
26	27	28	29	30

31	32	33	34	35
36	37	38	39	40
41	42	43	44	45
46	47	48	49	50
51	52	53	54	55
56	57	58	59	60

1

one

hour

What is an hour?

An hour is much longer than a minute:
it's **60 minutes**.
You can do a lot in an hour…

Like what?

You can draw a really big
picture and color it in.
You can play a game.
You can take an afternoon nap.
You can even bake a cake!

Like a
pound cake!

Let's bake one together so we can see
how long an hour is!
Put on your apron and turn the page…

How to make a pound cake

Ingredients

| 4 eggs | 1 c. (250 mL) sugar | 2 c. (500 mL) flour | 1 c. (250 mL) butter | 2 tsp. (10 mL) vanilla extract | ½ tsp. (2.5 mL) salt |

Ask an adult to help you preheat the oven to 350°F (180°C).

In a large mixing bowl:

1. Beat together the butter and sugar.

2. Crack the eggs and add them one at a time, blending well.

3. Add the vanilla and salt.

4. Gradually add the flour, beating just until combined.

5. Butter a round cake pan and pour in the batter.

6. Ask an adult to put the cake in the oven and set the timer for 45 minutes.

The cake is starting to bake, and the whole house smells so good!
Jacob and Lily use this time to put everything away.

They hear the DING of the timer. The cake is done!
Now Mom can take their masterpiece out of the oven.

They have to be patient for a few minutes longer while
the cake cools down. Finally Jacob and Lily can slice the cake…
but into how many pieces?

Two! One for you, and one for me!

Or maybe four! One for you, one for me, one for Mom, and one for Dad!

What a yummy-looking cake!
It took one whole hour to make it.
And it will only take five minutes to eat it!

1

one

day

What is a day?

It's much longer than an hour.

It's
24 hours.

A day is like a cake: you can cut it up into lots of different pieces!

A complete day is: morning, afternoon, evening, and night.

But how do you know what time it is?
There's too much time to count it all on your fingers!

That's why **clocks** were invented—to keep track of time.
Without clocks, you would never know if you are late or on time!

That's why we say...

Clocks are everywhere: in train stations,
at the post office, at city hall, and even at school.
There are clocks with numbers and clocks with hands.
And when you learn how to tell time, you can wear your very own watch!

The clock

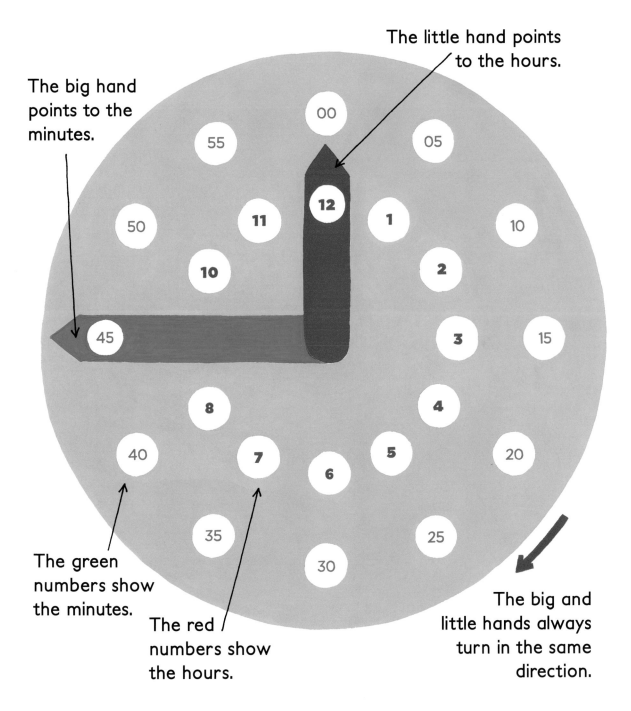

The little hand points to the hours.

The big hand points to the minutes.

The green numbers show the minutes.

The red numbers show the hours.

The big and little hands always turn in the same direction.

You can make your own clock to learn how it works!
Turn the page to see how.

Paper plate craft

What you need:

a paper plate   a marker   a glue stick   colored paper   a paper fastener

1. Cut a circle from the colored paper that is a bit smaller than the paper plate.

2. Glue the circle onto the plate so that your clock has a rim that's a different color from the face.

3. Write the hours in the proper places on the clock face.

4. Write the minutes on the rim.

5. Cut out an hour hand and a minute hand and fasten them to the center of the plate with the paper fastener.

Great job! You made your very own clock!

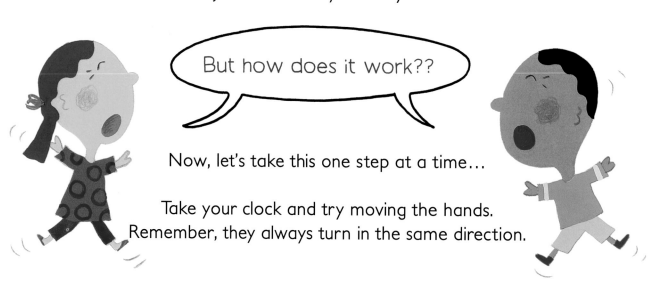

But how does it work??

Now, let's take this one step at a time…

Take your clock and try moving the hands. Remember, they always turn in the same direction.

Try moving the hour hand. That's the short hand.

It's 1 o'clock.

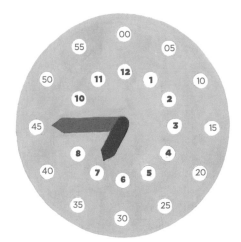

It's 2 o'clock.

To tell time correctly, first you read the number for the hour—the number that the short hand points to. Then you read the number for the minutes—the number that the long hand points to.

It's 4:10.

It's 7:45.

Try practicing on your own clock!

There's a neat little clock,
in the schoolroom it stands,
and it points to the time
with its two little hands.

The clock will be your guide all day long.
Soon you will figure out that there is a time for everything.
If you start to feel hungry, it must be time to eat.
If you feel tired, it must be bedtime.
If you are full of beans, it must be time to go out and play!

At noon, I eat macaroni.

At midnight, I'm in bed asleep...

zzzz

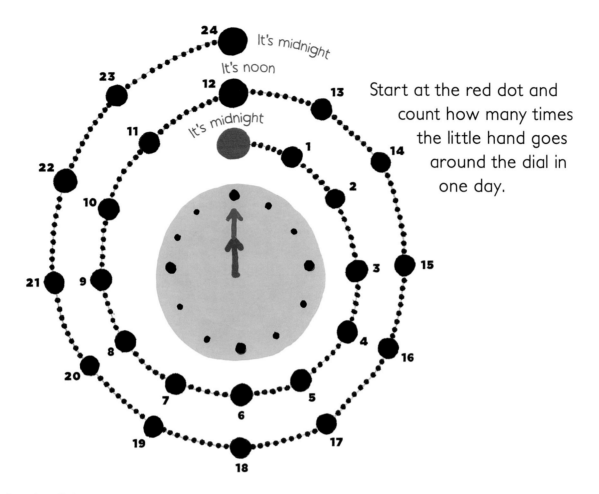

It's midnight

It's noon

It's midnight

Start at the red dot and count how many times the little hand goes around the dial in one day.

A day is divided into two sets of 12 hours—from midnight until noon, and from noon until the next midnight. The hours in the first part of the day are a.m. (before noon), and the hours in the second part of the day are p.m. (after noon).

a.m. and p.m. are short forms for "ante meridian" and "post meridian."

The word "meridian" comes from Latin and means "midday" or noon.

Lily's day

Morning

I wake up at 7:30 a.m., eat my breakfast, and get ready to go to school.

At school, I spend the morning learning to read, write, and count. At recess, I play with my friends.

It's noon, and I'm hungry! It's time to eat lunch so I'll have energy all afternoon.

Afternoon

It's 1:00 p.m. Time to go back to class!

This afternoon we're painting pictures and decorating them with stickers. It's fun!

It's 3:30 p.m. Yay! That's when Mom comes to pick me up!

Evening

I get home from school at around 4:00 p.m. Time for a yummy snack before I play.

Now it's 6:00 p.m.— dinnertime! Around the dinner table, we all talk about our days.

7:30 p.m. is bath time! I love bubble baths. I could stay in here for hours!

Night

I go to bed at 8:15 p.m. on a school night. I get to stay up later on the weekend.

Mom and Dad always read me a bedtime story before they kiss me goodnight.

At 9:00 p.m., I'm a sleepyhead. The sandman comes to visit, and I fall asleep…

Night

I'm sleeping, but the clock keeps on counting the passing time. It's 11:00 p.m.

While I'm in dreamland, the little hand keeps counting the hours and the big hand keeps counting the minutes.

Time never stops. But I do! I have to rest because tomorrow I'm going to school again…

Night

Tick tock, tick tock, ding! It's midnight! The start of a new day…

But it's still nighttime! 1:00 a.m., 2:00 a.m., 4:00 a.m., and I'm still fast asleep…

Morning

I wake up at 7:30 a.m., eat my breakfast, and get ready for school.

What time is it?

It's 11:00 a.m.

1

2

3

4

5

6

7

8

ANSWERS: 1: It's 11:40 p.m. 2: It's 4:30 p.m. 3: It's 8:15 p.m. 4: It's 2:00 p.m. 5: It's midnight. 6: It's noon. 7: It's 7:50 p.m. 8: It's 3:25 p.m.

27

1

one

week

What is a week?

One week
is
7 days.

Every day of the week has its own name.
There are days that you go to school, and days that you don't.
Do you know the days of the week?

Sunday
Monday
Tuesday
Wednesday
Thursday
Friday
Saturday

To help you remember, sing this rhyme to the tune of *Twinkle, Twinkle, Little Star.*

Sunday, Monday, Tuesday, too.
Wednesday, Thursday, just for you.
Friday, Saturday — that's the end.
Now let's say those days again!
Sunday, Monday, Tuesday, Wednesday,
Thursday, Friday, Saturday!

What child are you?

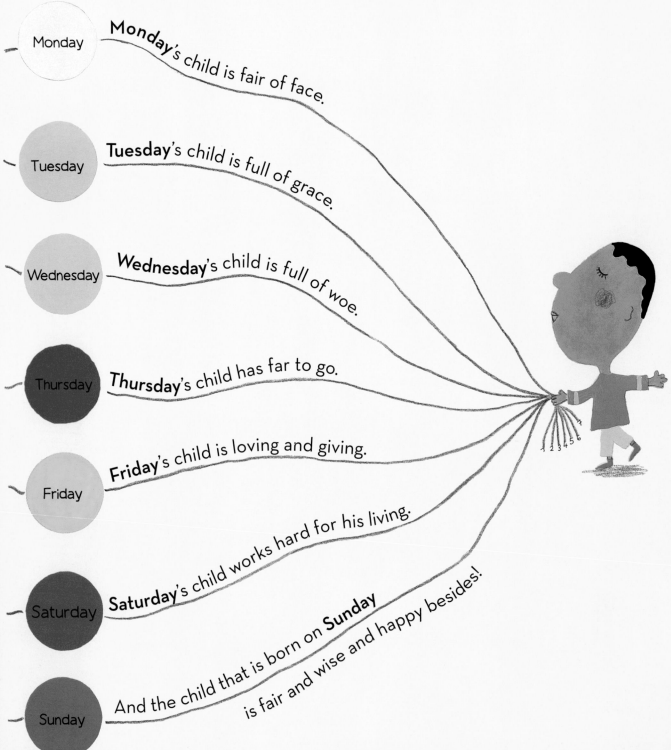

Monday

Monday's child is fair of face.

Tuesday

Tuesday's child is full of grace.

Wednesday

Wednesday's child is full of woe.

Thursday

Thursday's child has far to go.

Friday's child is loving and giving.

Friday

Saturday's child works hard for his living.

Saturday

And the child that is born on Sunday

is fair and wise and happy besides!

Sunday

Let's play with days!

1. What is the first day of the week?

2. What is the last day of the week?

3. Today is Saturday, and you don't have to go to school. What is the day before Saturday?

4. What is the day after Saturday?

> Today is the day that you are having right now.

> Yesterday was the day before today. Tomorrow is the day after today.

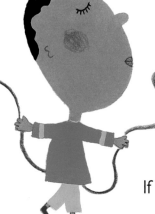

5. If your birthday is on a Thursday, what is the next day of the week?

6. If today is Monday, what is tomorrow? What was yesterday?

7. On Sunday, you call your friends to invite them to come over to your house in three days. What day will your friends come over?

ANSWERS: 1: Sunday is the first day of the week. 2: Saturday is the last day of the week. 3: Friday is the day before Saturday. 4: Sunday is the day after Saturday. 5: Friday is after Thursday. 6: Tomorrow is Tuesday and yesterday was Sunday. 7: Your friends will come over on Wednesday.

1

one

month

What is a month?

It's a little more than four weeks.
A month can have 28, 29, 30, or even 31 days.

Wow, a month is really long! Time keeps getting longer and longer...

And summer vacation is even longer than one month! It's at least two months long!

So clocks were invented to keep track of time, and all the days of the week have names. But how do we know what day of the month it is?

Quick, turn the page to find out!

Each day in a month is numbered
so that we know what day of the month it is:

from 1 to 31
or from 1 to 30
or from 1 to 29
or from 1 to 28

depending on how long the month is.

First you say the day of the week, then you say the number for the day of the month...

For example, you are coming over for an after-school snack on:

Friday,
the
18th

When you talk about the days in a month,
instead of using cardinal numbers, like

one, two, three, four, five...
1, 2, 3, 4, 5...

you use ordinal numbers, like

first, second, third, fourth, fifth...
1st, 2nd, 3rd, 4th, 5th...

What day of the month did you start reading this page?
Wednesday the 12th? Saturday the 27th?

Using the ordinal numbers below,
can you make up some more dates?

1st	2nd	3rd	4th	5th
6th	7th	8th	9th	10th
11th	12th	13th	14th	15th
16th	17th	18th	19th	20th
21st	22nd	23rd	24th	25th
26th	27th	28th	29th	30th
		31st		

1

one
year

What is a year?

It's
12 months
or
365 days.

Here are the names of all the months of the year:

January
February
March
April
May
June
July
August
September
October
November
December

The year starts on January 1st.

And the year ends 12 months later, on December 31st.

Lily and Jacob have a little secret to help you remember how many days there are in each month. So turn the page, and clench your fists…

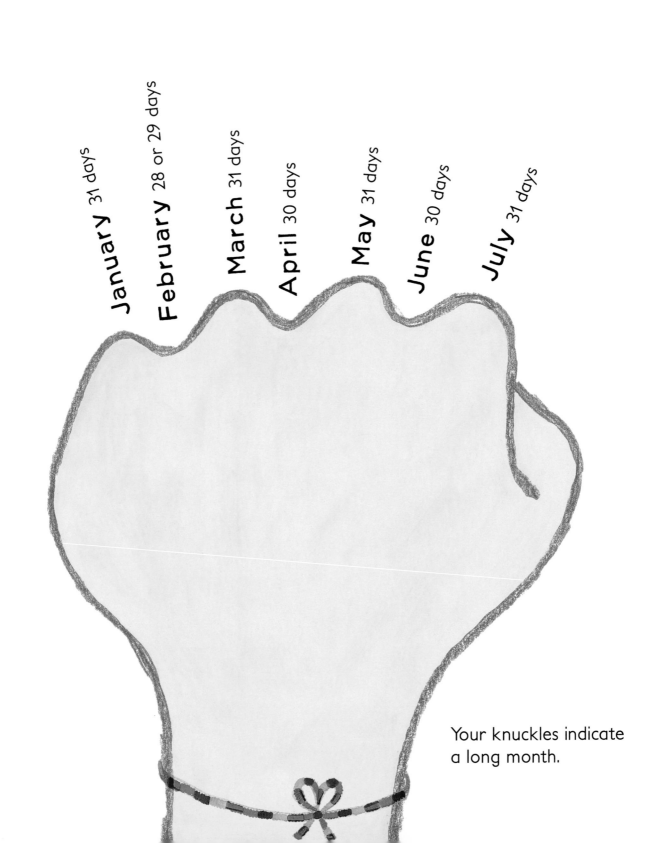

January 31 days

February 28 or 29 days

March 31 days

April 30 days

May 31 days

June 30 days

July 31 days

Your knuckles indicate a long month.

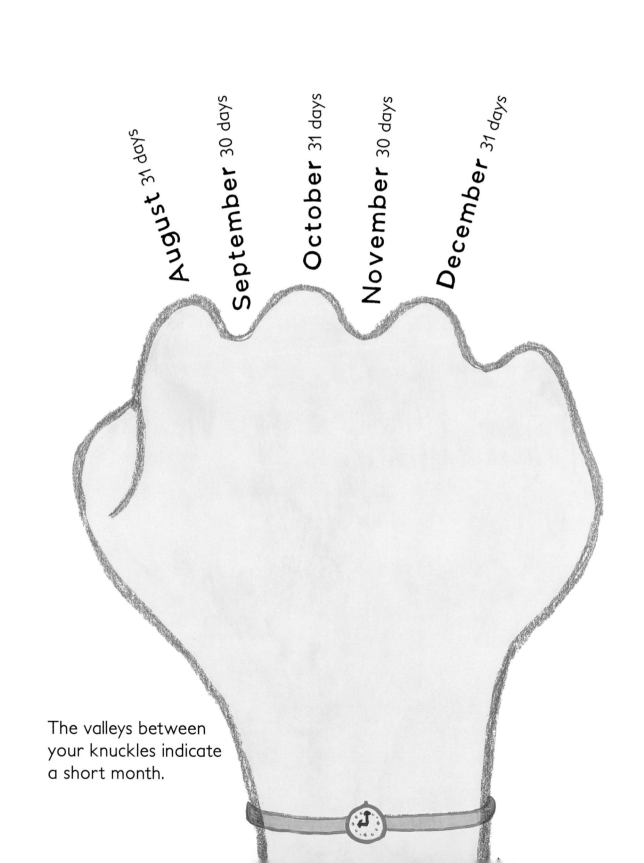

August 31 days

September 30 days

October 31 days

November 30 days

December 31 days

The valleys between your knuckles indicate a short month.

It's your birthday!

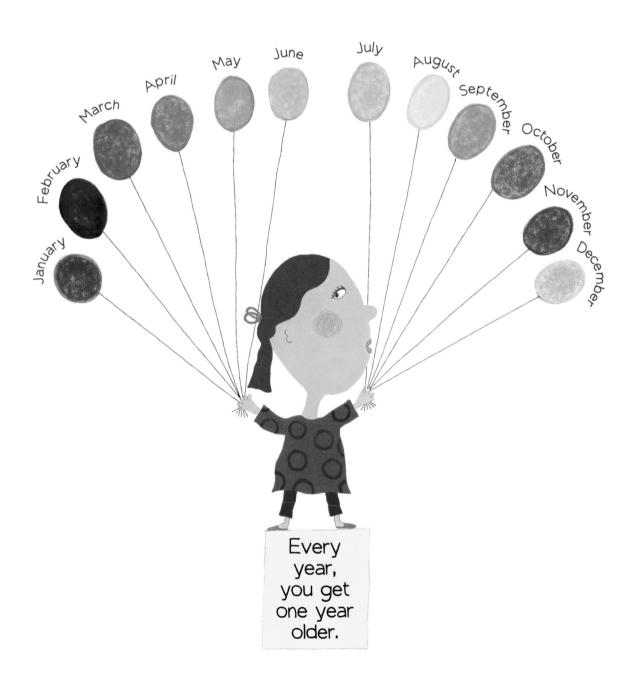

January
February
March
April
May
June
July
August
September
October
November
December

Every year, you get one year older.

Which balloon matches your birthday month?

A lot happens in one year.
There is a time for everything:
school time, vacation time, party time, birthday time.
Depending on where you live, there might be changes in the weather:
it might be sunny, cold, rainy, or snowy.

The year is shaped by the changing seasons.
In one year, there are
4 seasons.

Spring

Summer

Fall

Winter

The year and its seasons

Spring

March

April

May

Summer

June

July

August

Fall

September

October

November

Winter

December

January

February

Fashions for the four seasons

Which seasons are Lily and Jacob dressed for?

1

one

century

What is a century?

It's
100 **years**.

You can say 100 years, but you can also say a century.
How do you keep track of all that time?

So you don't get mixed up, calendars were invented.
All the years have been numbered.
Every calendar is filled with dates.

How do you read the date?

1 the day   2 the month   3 the number for the day of the month   4 the year

For example:

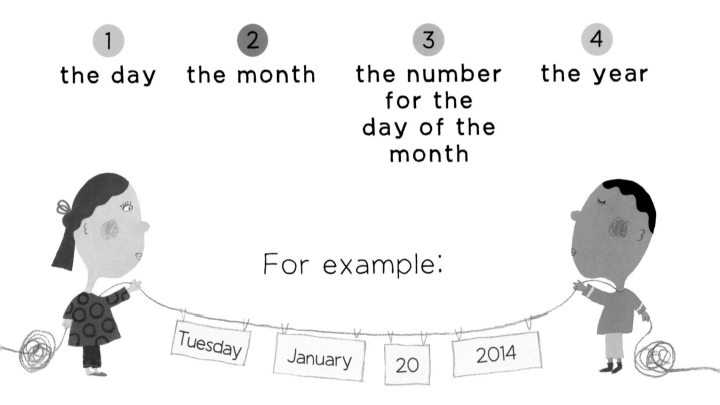

Tuesday   January   20   2014

When the 2014 calendar is finished, there will be another calendar for 2015, and another for 2016, and many more after that...

This is Lily's birthday.
How old is she?

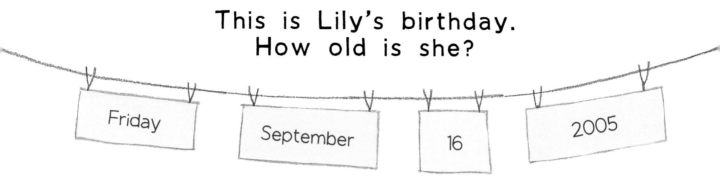

Friday   September   16   2005

This is Jacob's birthday.
How old is he?

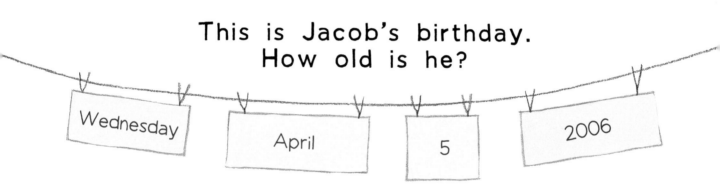

Wednesday   April   5   2006

When is your birthday? How old are you?

See how much time has passed since you were born?
As time passes, you grow up...

When one century ends,
another century begins
with
a new second,
a new minute,
a new hour,
a new day,
a new week,
a new month,
a new year...

Time never stops!

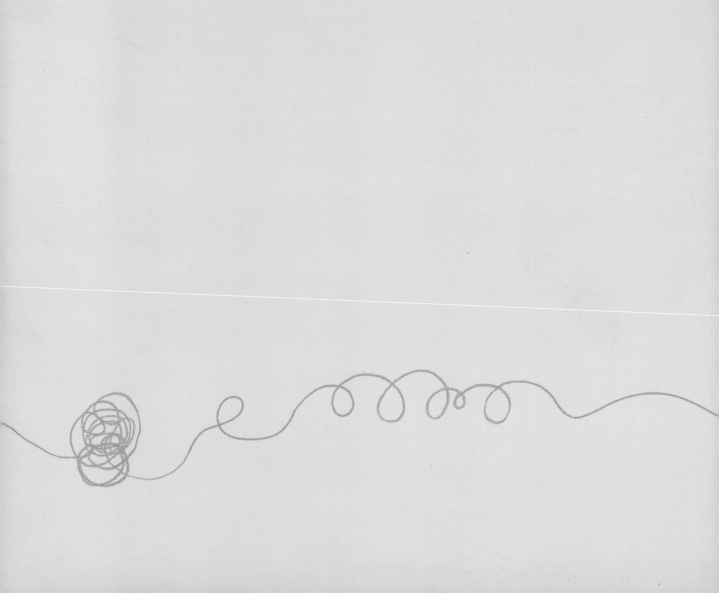